Face the Facts

Chemical and Biological Warfare

Adam Hibbert

Raintree

Chicago, Illinois

Printed and bound in China.
07 06 05 04 03
10 9 8 7 6 5 4 3 2 1

Library of Congress Cataloging-in-Publication Data:

Hibbert, Adam.
  Chemical and biological warfare / Adam Hibbert.
    v. cm. -- (Face the facts)
Includes bibliographical references and index.
Contents: History of chemical and biological warfare -- Chemical and
biological warfare today -- Arguments in CBW -- What is being done? --
CBW and you -- Facts and figures.
  ISBN 0-7398-6847-0
  1. Chemical warfare--Juvenile literature. 2. Biological
warfare--Juvenile literature. [1. Chemical warfare. 2. Biological
warfare.] I. Title. II. Series.
  UG447.M344 2004
  358'.3--dc21
                           2003002064

Acknowledgments
The publisher would like to thank the following for permission to reproduce photographs:
Pp. 4, 34, 36, 43 EPA/Press Association; p. 5 Bodleian Library/AKG London; p. 6 Josh Reynolds/ImageWorks/Topham Picturepoint; p. 8 Paul Almasy/Corbis; p. 9 Richard S. Green/Science Photo Library; pp. 10–11 Bettman/Corbis; p. 12 Sally Morgan/Ecoscene/Corbis; pp. 13, 17 British Library/AKG London; pp. 15, 31 Hulton Archive; p. 16, 24 Reuters/Popperfoto; pp. 18–19, 25 Alexei Sazonov/Associated Press; pp. 20–21 Ed Kashi/Corbis; pp. 23, 39 ImageWorks/Topham Picturepoint; pp. 26–27 Ron Sanford/Corbis; p. 28 Bolivar Arellano/NY Post/Sygma/Corbis; p. 29 Reuters/Popperfoto; p. 32 Cristina Pedrazzini/Science Photo Library; P. 33 Jean-Loup Charmet/Science Photo Library; pp. 35, 41 Mike Hutchings/Reuters/Popperfoto; p. 40 Toshiyuki Aizawa/Reuters; p. 44 Canadian Press/Press Association; p. 47 Houston Scott/Sygma/Corbis; p. 48 ImageState/Alamy; p. 51 Nick Cobbing/David Hoffman Photo Library/Alamy.

Cover photograph: Digital Vision.

Some words are shown in bold, **like this,** you can find out what they mean by looking in the glossary.

Contents

Introduction

Today's battles are fought with very different weapons from the ones used in the past. Here, rioters and police wear masks to protect themselves from tear gas, a type of chemical weapon.

Most weapons, from bows and arrows to machine guns, work by causing a direct injury to an enemy's body. Swords, arrows, and bullets all pierce the skin, causing bleeding or damaging a vital body part. But chemical and biological weapons are different. Instead of inflicting simple, direct injuries, they cause chemical reactions or diseases that attack the body. In most cases, they harm every person in an area, not just enemy soldiers.

Chemical weapons are created by mixing chemicals together to make poisonous solids, liquids, or gases that react with parts of the body, causing severe pain and often death. Biological weapons (or **bioweapons**) are made using the germs that cause disease in humans, animals, or plants. These germs can also be bred to create "super-bugs" that may disable or kill anyone infected with them. Although these two **agents** are made in very different ways, they create very similar problems for society.

Controlling the weapons

Over the last 100 years, international organizations, such as the **United Nations (UN),** have laid down rules for war. These rules are made to try to keep wars from causing too much damage. The UN rules (see page 35) state that chemical and biological weapons are totally prohibited unless their use is for peaceful, protective purposes. Certain chemical agents can be used to control riots and enforce law and order, but not in a war situation. However, these rules do not work with people such as **terrorists,** who deliberately break the law and use violence to draw attention to their cause.

Chemical and biological weapons **(CBWs)** are often called Weapons of Mass Destruction (or WMDs) because they cause widespread harm, killing many innocent people as well as enemy soldiers. However, WMDs also include **nuclear weapons.** CBW warfare is different from nuclear warfare, because it can be used by small groups or individuals. Nuclear technology is difficult and expensive, limiting its use to countries with the proper technological resources, but CBWs can be used in **guerrilla** warfare or in terrorist campaigns.

This medieval painting shows knights fighting with swords. Until very recently, people have mainly used weapons that caused direct physical damage to an enemy soldier's body.

Types of Weapon

Chemical weapons are usually produced by scientists, who mix different chemicals together in a laboratory to produce poisonous solids, liquids, or gases. Biological weapons are harder to make than chemical weapons. Scientists cannot yet build a new **organism** (a living thing, such as a germ), so they have to find one that is already deadly, and then find ways to make it as powerful as possible.

Biological weapons

An effective **bioweapon** has to be able to infect its human targets easily, to reproduce quickly, to spread between targets, and to kill or disable people who are infected.

At the same time, it should not be too good at these tasks, or it might get out of control and destroy the users as well as the victims. For this reason, most bioweapons developed by countries have been highly infectious (easy to catch), but not highly contagious, which means they do not spread very easily between people. Anthrax is a good example of a biological weapon that is very infectious but not contagious.

Chemical weapons

There are at least four types of chemical weapon. The first type is fairly simple. It consists of chemical **agents,** such as pepper spray and CS gas (a gas that smells like pepper, but is even more irritating). These chemicals make their human targets helpless for a short time. They irritate the eyes—which is why they are sometimes known as "tear gases"—and cause people to have trouble breathing, but their effects wear off relatively quickly.

A masked protester hurls a canister of tear gas back at a line of police who had thrown it into the crowd.

The second type of chemical is more dangerous. These are substances, such as **mustard gas,** that "burn" the skin and eyes, causing painful blisters and blindness. They are designed to slow an enemy army down by wounding thousands of soldiers. However, although the damage from these chemicals is long-lasting, they only kill about one percent of their targets.

The third type of chemical weapon is made from lung-damaging chemicals that can be deadly when they are breathed in. When people breathe in these chemicals, the linings of their lungs produce fluid to protect themselves, and if the lungs fill with fluid, the victim literally drowns. Chlorine gas, which was used in World War I, is an example of a lung-damaging chemical.

The fourth type of chemical weapon is the most complex and the most dangerous. **Nerve agents** penetrate the skin and lung linings, destroying nerves and causing victims to lose control of their bodies. In most cases, nerve agents can cause enough damage to stop the heartbeat. An example of a nerve agent is tabun, which was used in the Iran-Iraq War of 1980–1988.

Bioweapons

There are two main types of **bioweapon, viruses** and **bacteria**. Viruses are the simplest forms of life—tiny particles that need to steal from more complex life forms in order to grow and reproduce. They take over **cells** in a plant or an animal, making millions of copies of themselves. Bacteria are very simple, single-celled **organisms** that are found everywhere on Earth, including the human gut.

The scars on the face of this Afghan boy, photographed in the 1970s, show that he has survived a smallpox infection. Smallpox was finally stamped out in 1980, but it could still be used as a biological weapon.

Deadly viruses

Viruses that may be used in **CBW** warfare include smallpox and **VHFs.** Smallpox was a deadly disease around the world until a global health campaign finally stamped it out in 1980. At least two laboratories, one in Russia and one in the United States, kept samples of smallpox for research. The U.S. Center for Disease Control has about 500 different strains of smallpox in a freezer to help scientists create **vaccines** to use in an emergency.

The initials VHF stand for Viral Hemorrhagic Fever. These viruses cause heavy bleeding and fevers, and often lead to death. The VHF family of viruses are very infectious. They include Ebola, Marburg, and Hanta. All of them cause terrible internal bleeding, and even bleeding from skin pores and the eyes. The natural version of the Ebola virus is widespread in Africa. It is often deadly, although it can be survived with proper medical care. However, a military version might be even more dangerous. It is not known if any country has succeeded in creating a VHF weapon.

Harmful bacteria

Very few bacteria are deadly to humans, but two types of bacteria that are used in research into bioweapons are anthrax and **botulinum.** Anthrax is the most famous bacteria in bioweapons research. Though harmful to cattle, it is not normally powerful enough to kill a fit human being, unless it is inhaled as a cloud of microscopic dust particles. Botulinum is not deadly in itself, but produces a poison called botulinum **toxin,** which is the most powerful **nerve agent** known to science. Other bacteria that have been used as weapons include bubonic plague, swine fever, and glanders, a bacteria that infects and kills horses.

The highly dangerous Ebola virus is a type of VHF. It is seen here through a very powerful microscope.

CBWs on the Battlefield

CBWs can be very hard to deliver to an enemy in large quantities. In practice, four methods of delivery have been used in battle. The first method involves waiting until the wind is blowing toward the enemy and then releasing CBW gases or dust into the air. But wind direction is hard to predict. If the wind changes, CBWs can be carried back to the troops that are using the weapons. The second method is to fly over enemy positions and drop breakable bottles of CBW material. The third is to fire shells filled with CBW material, which break open on impact. The fourth is to load the **agent** into a large spray tank, similar to a large-scale aerosol can, and attach the can to the underside of an aircraft. In this way very large areas can be covered with the agent. The spray method was used to clear large areas of jungle, using chemical **defoliants,** during the Vietnam War.

In World War I, **mustard gas** was often carried toward enemy soldiers by the wind. In this photograph, U.S. soldiers act out the horror of a gas attack to prepare other soldiers for battle.

CBWs and the weather

The weather poses big challenges for CBW warfare. Biological weapons normally need a particular temperature and moisture level to remain active. The wrong weather or even sunlight can kill the germs. However, testing of biological agents in a remote part of Scotland (Gruinard Island) showed that anthrax, one of the most effective and long-lasting biological warfare agents, can remain in a weakened form in the soil for a period of up to 50 years. Some chemical weapons stay active longer in cold weather, and this may make it dangerous to capture territory abandoned by an enemy after a successful chemical weapons attack.

Protection and transportation

CBW warfare is not simply about having the technology to make a weapon. Military commanders have to be able to defend against CBW attacks as well. They need instruments to check what is in the air, CBW-proof suits and gas masks to protect soldiers, airtight vehicles and buildings for the victims, and medical support to treat **casualties.** Troops need to be well trained, and may be given drugs or **vaccines** to protect them. Each of these measures costs money and time, and the use of drugs and vaccines may expose troops to new dangers.

Weapons are normally made a long way from the battlefield and then shipped to it. For CBWs, special ships or planes are needed to do this safely. If they are not dropped from planes as bombs, CBWs need to be stored where they can be reached if needed. As with all **ammunition** stores, this is dangerous since enemy fire could break one open. In the case of CBWs, if the active agents are released in the wrong place, an army could be poisoned or cut off from its supplies and its lines of retreat.

CBWs Through the Ages

Sometimes harmless-looking plants can be used as deadly weapons. The ancient Greeks used the root of the hellebore plant to poison the water supplies of enemy cities.

The first well-documented example of **CBW** warfare appears in history books about World War I. But chemical and biological weapons were used much earlier than that. Some of the evidence is hard to be certain about, because people often used CBWs without any scientific understanding of how they worked.

Humans have known about **toxins** in nature for thousands of years. Some native people, such as the Wai-Wai of Guyana, in South America, still harvest poisonous plants and catch poisonous animals to use their toxins on arrows or darts for hunting. Poisons like these were probably used against other humans in early warfare.

The ancient Greeks used poisonous plants as chemical weapons. They put roots from the hellebore plant into the water supply of cities to force the defenders to abandon the city. They also burned sulphur when the wind was blowing toward an enemy army. This created noxious, choking clouds and disabled the enemy troops.

Plague attack

The most famous early use of a biological weapon was in 1346. At this time a terrible disease—the bubonic plague, also known as the "Black Death"—was spreading from China toward Europe, carried by merchants along the trading routes. When the plague reached present-day Ukraine, it infected an army of **Tartars** who were trying to reclaim the city of Kaffa from Italian traders. Instead of burying their dead, the Tartars threw the plague victims over the city walls, to infect the Italians. Some surviving traders managed to escape from the city, but they carried the deadly disease with them back to Italy. The Black Death was extremely infectious and contagious. It spread amazingly quickly, killing almost a third of Europe's population within five years.

This picture from a medieval manuscript shows people suffering from the Black Death. Some of the victims of the Black Death were used as deadly biological weapons by the Tartars in the siege of Kaffa.

Spreading smallpox

Another cruel use of a biological weapon took place in Canada in 1763. British soldiers fighting the Native Americans smeared pus from smallpox victims on blankets and then sent the blankets as a gift to their enemies. The disease spread very rapidly through the Native American people. British troops were given an early type of **vaccination** to protect them from this deadly "weapon."

World War I (1914–1918)

During World War I, warfare changed dramatically. New technologies—submarines, tanks, machine guns, aircraft, high explosives, and poison gases—all provided new ways to fight a war. Most importantly, nations at war began to think in terms of killing large numbers of the enemy at once.

At 5:00 P.M. on April 22, 1915, fighting at Ypres, Belgium, was drawing to an end for the day when troops fighting for the **Allies** noticed a weird, greenish cloud approaching them from the German **trenches.** They were seeing the first serious gas attack of the war. The chlorine gas blinded and choked the men who breathed it in. By 5:30 P.M., the Allies were forced to abandon a 2-mile (3-kilometer) stretch of their trenches. Unprotected German troops followed behind the cloud of gas, capturing several villages and big guns. It was a dramatic introduction to the power of chemical warfare. The Allied troops were shocked and frightened.

Several countries that were not involved in the war spoke out against this cruel use of gas. But by the end of the war, all sides would be using chlorine and other, more deadly gases. Soon gas masks were invented to protect soldiers, as well as better ways to deliver the gas in shells rather than just releasing it into the wind. But gas was not a reliable weapon, and its effects were so horrible that it was banned after the war. Roughly 100,000 soldiers were killed by gas in World War I and another 900,000 or so were badly injured, with permanently burned and scarred lungs that made breathing difficult for the rest of their lives.

British soldiers, blinded by a mustard gas attack in 1918, form a line to follow a man who can see.

14

"Men marched asleep. Many had lost their boots,
But limped on, blood-shod. All went lame, all blind;
Drunk with fatigue; deaf even to the hoots
Of gas-shells dropping softly behind.

Gas! Gas! Quick, boys! An ecstasy of fumbling,
Fitting the clumsy helmets just in time,
But someone still was yelling out and stumbling
And floundering like a man in fire or lime.
Dim through the misty panes and thick green light,
As under a green sea, I saw him drowning.
In all my dreams, before my helpless sight,
He plunges at me, guttering, choking, drowning."

Lines describing a gas attack during the World War I, from the poem "Dulce et Decorum est," by the British soldier and poet Wilfred Owen

World War II (1939–1945)

In the years following World War I, scientists in many countries carried out research into new forms of poison gas. But during World War II, the threat of **retaliation** was enough to keep these new weapons in storage, because neither side wanted to risk the possibility that the other might have a "super-weapon." Even so, thousands were injured or killed by chemical **agents,** when storage or transport tanks leaked or broke open during bombing raids.

In 1943 a ship belonging to the **Allies,** the *John Harvey*, was blown open at Bari, Italy, killing 69 people and disabling hundreds. The ship had been carrying a top-secret shipment of **mustard gas** to the battlefront. The gas leaked, and all the officers who knew the secret were killed trying to stop the gas from spreading. This meant that no warning could be given to survivors on the ship, or to the people of Bari, or to any medical staff who could have treated them.

A London air-raid warden fits a young boy with a gas mask in 1939 to protect him against possible gas attacks on the city. Gas masks like this, which were specially designed for children, were known as "Mickey Mouse" masks.

The Holocaust

The most horrific use of chemicals ever known took place during World War II, when Hitler's Nazi party attempted to murder millions of Jewish citizens. This terrible massacre came to be known as the Holocaust. Jews and others, such as Romanies (also called gypsies) and the disabled—were rounded up into **concentration camps,** where the Nazis forced them into slave labor or gassed them to death.

Zyklon B was a German **pesticide** that was used to kill insects such as **lice.** It was based on prussic acid, which is a deadly poison. At first, the Nazis used Zyklon B to control lice among the prisoners, but then they began using it to gas Jewish people to death, hundreds at a time. By the end of World War II, roughly six million Jews had been killed. It is impossible to prove how many were gassed, and how many were shot, starved, or worked to death. However, it is known that Zyklon B was used to kill more than a million people at Auschwitz concentration camp in Poland.

Soldiers from the **Soviet Union** display canisters of deadly Zyklon B, found in Auschwitz concentration camp at the end of World War II.

17

The Cold War (1945–1990)

U.S. Air Force planes spray Agent Orange over jungle and farmland during the Vietnam War. Agent Orange is a defoliant, which destroys crops, plants, and trees.

Two main powers emerged from World War II—the United States and the **Soviet Union (USSR).** Both countries had major **CBW** research programs. At the end of World War II, the United States had gained new CBW expertise from Germany when German scientists fled to America, in order to avoid being captured by the Soviet troops who were marching through Germany. The United States also gained valuable information from Great Britain, as British scientists provided full details of their experiments into biological warfare.

The United States and the Soviet Union had different ideas about how the post-war world should be run. They battled for control of the world, but never fought in open conflict against each other. Instead the two countries supported opposite sides in wars in other parts of the world. This period of hostility lasted

from the end of World War II to the start of the 1990s and is called the **Cold War.** During the Cold War, neither side could be sure whether the other would use CBWs, so both sides did research. They also shared some CBW knowledge and technology with the other countries that they supported.

While the United States and the Soviet Union were carrying out this research, the British army had learned to use weedkillers to make it easier to fight rebels in the jungles of Malaysia. The weedkillers destroyed large areas of jungle, exposing enemy soldiers to attacks from the air. U.S. scientists learned from the British and developed chemicals, such as Agent Orange. This is a highly poisonous **defoliant** that was used to strip away vast areas of jungle during the war between U.S. troops and **communist** rebels in Vietnam.

Problems and slowdown

In the United States, CBW research was carried out on volunteers at Camp Detrick (now Fort Detrick). The details of most of these tests are still classified (kept secret), but the U.S. military claims that it gained useful new knowledge about defending soldiers from CBW attacks. At the same time, **delivery systems** for CBWs were tested at Dugway, Utah. In 1968, over 6,000 sheep were killed near the base at Dugway when a test aircraft's delivery system for the **nerve agent** VX jammed open, causing a deadly cloud to drift for miles outside the target area. Then, in 1969, when scientists found traces of a **bioweapon** in blood samples from wildlife around Dugway, voters became much less tolerant of CBW research. President Nixon announced that the United States was stopping its research and development into biological warfare, and during the late 1960s and early 1970s the United States began to dismantle its **offensive** program and started to destroy its CBWs.

In the late 1980s, the Soviet Union fell apart and the Cold War came to an end. This marked the end of one chapter in the history of CBW warfare.

The Iran-Iraq War (1980-1988)

Toward the end of the **Cold War,** there was a major case of a country using **CBWs** in open warfare. This was the Iran-Iraq War, which lasted from 1980 to 1988. In 1979 a revolution in Iran put a fanatic Islamic leader into power. The countries of the West and the **Soviet Union** were both concerned about this new Islamic power in the region, so each in its own way helped Iraq to fight a war against Iran. Some of this help is on public record, such as 21 anthrax samples shipped to Iraq from Fort Detrick and a germ "library" in Maryland. Iraq used CBWs in the war as early as 1983. In one battle in 1986, the Iraqis used **mustard gas** and the **nerve agent** tabun, killing up to 10,000 of the enemy.

Mustard gas and nerve gas were both used against Iran's foot soldiers. Iraq also used chemical bombs and **missiles** against Iranian war headquarters. At the very end of the war, there was a battle for control of the town of Halabja in northern Iraq. The town was held by rebel **Kurds,** who wanted to use the war to free their region from the control of the Iraqi government. Many thousands of rebel fighters and their families were poisoned in a massive Iraqi CBW attack.

Kurdish guerrillas inspect an unexploded chemical bomb dropped by Iraqi planes on the rebel town of Halabja in 1988.

Some experts believe that this terrible event, together with Iraq's new long-range missiles, convinced the leaders of Iran that they should make peace with Iraq. The Iranians feared that Iraq was now capable of striking the Iranian capital city, Tehran, with chemical weapons. **Bioweapons** had been too difficult for Iraq to perfect, but research was well under way and the Iranians were afraid of what might happen in the future.

The technology that Iraq gained during the war was not forgotten afterward. Top-secret research continued in Iraq after the war, leading the **UN** to become concerned that Iraq might use these weapons again, perhaps against Israel or even on its own citizens. In 1990 Iraq invaded its neighbor, Kuwait. UN forces drove Iraq out of Kuwait in 1991, and the UN demanded that Iraq destroy all its CBWs and end its CBW research. By 2002, the UN was still not sure that Iraq, led by Saddam Hussein, had given up CBWs. An American-led military force invaded Iraq in 2003 to **disarm** Saddam's **regime.**

Continued Problems

By the end of the 20th century, it seemed that the threat of a large-scale war using **CBWs** was fading, but a new challenge had taken its place. The biggest impact of CBW warfare at the start of the 21st century was the huge task of cleaning up the mess created in the previous century.

Cleaning up

With the growth of environmental awareness, it is now illegal to dump CBWs at sea, as was done after 1945. Also, the collapse of the **Soviet Union** has left Russia too poor to invest in safe disposal of CBW stockpiles. This leaves a massive task for other countries in the world. Some countries have built special factories to destroy CBWs, and a few, such as the United States, Germany, and Sweden, have given Russia money to help it build disposal factories. The work of safe disposal will take several decades, and the risk of leaks and accidents will continue until all CBWs are destroyed.

Casualties of CBW

At the same time as countries are trying to destroy old CBWs, the world also has to handle the effects of previous CBW warfare on humans and their environment. The **defoliant** used in the Vietnam War, Agent Orange, has harmed or disabled as many as one million Vietnamese citizens, as well as U.S. troops and their children. Agent Orange has been linked with a type of diabetes, disabilities in babies, cancers, and miscarriages. Some governments now pay their war **veterans** extra money to help them meet the cost of these injuries.

Case study Dangerous bombs

CBWs from World War I still threaten northern Europe. Shells containing **mustard gas** and other poisons are often found by people, such as farmers and builders, who disturb the ground where battles were once fought. When the shells are discovered they must be taken to safe collection points. In 2001 the town of Vimy in France had to be **evacuated** when a collection point containing 173 tons of these 85-year-old bombs was found to be unsafe because some of the bombs had leaked. Fortunately no one was harmed.

Still in use?

The use and development of chemical and biological weapons is not just a thing of the past. About 65 countries have promised to destroy all their stocks over the next two decades, but many are still researching CBWs to keep their defense technology up to date. No large military power would be eager to end its CBW program while the technology still exists in other parts of the world.

False alarms?

Countries that are involved in wars often make the claim that their enemy has used CBW warfare to gain public sympathy. North Korea, Iraq, and Cuba have each blamed the United States for outbreaks of crop-damaging insects in their countries. Good scientific proof has not been found for any of these cases, and very few people believe them to be true.

Leftover Agent Orange in Vietnam causes birth defects in thousands of children each year. These two Vietnamese boys are both victims of Agent Orange.

CBWs and Terrorism

In the 21st century, one of the greatest threats of **CBW** warfare may come from **terrorists.** After the **Cold War,** the number of terrorist attacks fell steadily as many conflicts came to an end. However, in recent years terror attacks have become more random (not directed at a specific enemy) and more deadly. In the past, terrorists had usually pinpointed "enemy" soldiers or politicians, for example, by bombing army barracks where soldiers lived. But by 2001, their targets were often ordinary **civilians.** This change has made CBW warfare by terrorists a real risk since the danger to innocent lives appears to have become less of a concern to terrorists.

A terrorist weapon

The first major case of a random terrorist CBW attack happened in 1995, in Japan. There, the powerful religious **cult** Aum Shinrikyo used its wealth to make a **nerve agent** called sarin. Scientists working for the cult did secret tests on animals in Australia before releasing the gas in Tokyo's subway system. Twelve people died and over 1,000 were hospitalized as a result of the attack. By luck, the sarin gas made for this mission was weaker than anything the cult had made before; otherwise several thousands more people could have been killed.

Japanese workers remove drums full of **toxic** chemicals from the Aum Shinrikyo laboratory following a police raid on the cult's headquarters.

衝雲・逆水厳禁 扱

三塩化

日本曹達株式

An antiterrorist weapon

In October 2002, 40 terrorists from Chechnya, a rebel province in southern Russia, held about 750 people hostage inside a theater in the Russian city of Moscow. They demanded an end to Russia's military rule of Chechnya and threatened to kill all the hostages if the Russian government did not agree to their demands. After three days, Russian security forces stormed the theater, using a knockout gas to stop the terrorists from killing everyone. The gas was very effective, but 129 hostages died from the side effects of the gas when they became unable to breathe. The Russian government was criticized for using the gas, despite rescuing some 700 hostages. CBW warfare had changed once more; this time it was used in the battle to fight terrorism.

Russian Interior Ministry troops take up their positions outside the Moscow theater, before storming the building using an anesthetic gas.

What gas?

The Russian government's use of gas against the Chechen hostage-takers surprised the world. At first, no one knew what the gas might be, and this caused fear that medical staff would not be able to deal with casualties in the best way. But the Russian authorities told doctors to treat survivors as if they had taken too much of an opium-based drug, such as heroin. After several days, the Russian authorities said that they had used a type of anesthetic, a gas used by doctors to put people to sleep during surgery. Because its security forces had used a medical gas, Russia had not broken any laws about researching or using chemical weapons.

Anthrax Attacks

Following the **terrorist** attacks in New York and Washington, D.C., on September 11, 2001, there was a series of anthrax attacks in the United States. In late September, someone mailed anthrax to journalists and politicians. The first two letters contained anthrax particles that were too small to float free of the paper and infect many people. But two more letters contained particles that formed a dust cloud that could be inhaled. In total, five people died, including two postal workers. As a precaution, roughly 30,000 people at high risk were treated with **antibiotics** to protect them against the deadly effects of anthrax.

Anthrax research

The anthrax attacks in the U.S. postal system alerted the public to the danger of **CBWs.** If the anthrax attacker had used better technology, thousands or even millions of people might have been infected. Stocks of antibiotics would have run out, and tens of thousands could have died. The FBI studied the risks from anthrax attackers and considered a range of possible **delivery systems.** One possible delivery system investigated by the FBI was crop-dusting aircraft. These planes have spray tanks that could be filled with anthrax. In September 2001, the United States's 3,000 crop dusters were not allowed to fly while the FBI carried out their investigation.

In the months following the terrorist attacks on the United States in September 2001, some people feared that crop-dusting planes could be used to spread anthrax.

Fortunately U.S. security forces were soon able to calm some of the public's fears. The FBI found that anthrax could be grown using normal industrial equipment. However, there were three major reasons why a full-scale anthrax attack would be less likely than had been feared. First, the basic equipment needed would cost about $1 million and was not freely available in most countries. Second, terrorists would need a special breed of anthrax, a type found only in top-security military research labs. Third, only a few military scientists around the world knew how to process anthrax into its most dangerous form, dust. Even the wealthy and highly skilled Japanese Aum Shinrikyo **cult** (see page 24) had failed to make it.

It was also found that crop dusters were not as risky as feared. Pilots need extreme skill to fly them, especially when the spray tanks are full. They would also need some very complicated changes to be able to spray a fine cloud of anthrax dust. Sprayed as a liquid, anthrax would be relatively harmless to humans, although it might harm farm animals grazing on **contaminated** grass.

Real and Imagined Fears

Chemical and biological warfare appeals to **terrorists** not just because of its destructive potential, but also because even the idea of these weapons causes fear. The difficult science of **CBWs** leaves most people unable to make sense of the risks for themselves. This public fear may become more damaging to a country than an actual attack. In order to show that they are protecting their country, politicians may have to make extra laws, and find money for a wide range of security measures. The security measures may cause delay, inconvenience, and even new risks.

Across the world, in the weeks following the attacks of September 11, 2001, hundreds of businesses, transportation systems, and schools had their usual schedules interrupted by anthrax hoaxes and false alarms. Buildings were sealed for hours before people could return to work. Airports and railroad stations had to be closed down. It has been impossible to add up all the hours of productivity that were lost around the world as a result of these scares.

Emergency service workers in New York practice dealing with a **nerve agent** attack. Rehearsals like this are very important, but they can also cause alarm.

Sterilizing mail

In the United States, every piece of mail sent to government offices now has to pass through a machine that **sterilizes** it. Any **bacteria** in the mail is destroyed by this machine. However, there is some evidence that this "clean" mail is riskier for postal workers to handle than normal mail. The process dries out the paper, making it dustier and more likely to irritate the skin and lungs. In addition, the extra step in the process of mail delivery adds time and cost to postal services.

> **❝Had we not hit that target [the Al Shifa factory] and had bin Laden used chemical weapons in a terrorist attack, I don't know how we could have looked the American people in the face.❞**
>
> Sandy Berger, U.S. National Security Adviser, justifying the attack on the Al Shifa drug factory in 1998

Employees inspect the ruins of the Al Shifa medicine factory, which was destroyed by U.S. missiles in the mistaken belief that it was a chemical weapons factory.

Dual-use items

There are other sorts of costs created by combatting CBW terrorism. CBW makers often use equipment and materials that have a **dual use:** a military one and an innocent **civilian** use, such as making medicines. Controlling dual-use items can help to prevent the creation of deadly CBWs, but can also delay progress on vital social and medical projects. In one case, concern over dual use led to disaster. In 1998 the United States launched a **missile** attack on the Al Shifa medicine factory in Khartoum (East Africa), because it feared that the factory was manufacturing CBWs to be used in terror campaigns against the United States. However, CBWs were not being manufactured there, and the attack knocked out one of East Africa's best resources in the life-or-death struggle against malaria and other diseases.

Are CBWs Worse than Other Weapons?

CBW warfare is usually considered more horrible than other types of warfare. However, it is not always easy to understand why this is the case. All kinds of warfare cause terrible suffering and death, so why are CBWs considered to be so much worse?

Killing civilians

One argument against CBW warfare is that **civilians** should not be killed in war. CBWs will kill or injure anyone—soldier, civilian, or child—who is exposed to them. However, almost every war in the last 150 years has involved civilians, either killing them or destroying their lives in other ways.

Since the end of World War II, nations have tried to avoid killing civilians in warfare. But this is almost impossible to avoid in industrial societies with large cities. If CBW warfare is opposed on the grounds that it would cause the large-scale killing of innocent civilians, it could be argued that there should also be a ban on the use of high-flying aircraft to drop bombs on cities, since these also cause countless civilian deaths.

Excessive force

Many people would agree that it is morally acceptable for individuals to use force to defend themselves against an attack. But this self-defense should not involve the use of unnecessary force. For example, it is not usually right to respond to being punched by using a knife or a gun. This idea can be applied to large-scale warfare, as well. It can be argued that the disabilities suffered by people in a CBW attack are much worse than the usual injuries that soldiers might expect to risk in battle. However, this argument against the use of CBWs needs to be balanced against the effects of other types of weapon, such as **fuel-air explosives,** which also cause terrible lung damage.

A different attitude

Most people find the use of CBWs unacceptable because it reflects a particularly uncaring attitude to the victims of an attack. While it is possible to argue that the use of **conventional weapons** shows some respect for the enemy soldiers' ability to fight back, users of CBWs are treating their victims as if they were less than human. The Nazis' use of poison gas in the **concentration camps** is especially shocking because the prisoners were not treated like human beings, but destroyed like fleas or **lice.**

Causing disease

Throughout human history people have made enormous efforts to fight disease and heal the sick. In all cultures healing and caring for the sick are viewed as significant human virtues. Because of these attitudes toward disease, using a weapon that deliberately causes disease and sickness seems especially wrong.

CBWs are not the only weapons that cause large-scale destruction. This photograph shows part of London, badly damaged by bombs during World War II.

Is CBW Research Justified?

Scientific knowledge cannot just be forgotten, and people today have to live with the fact of **CBW** warfare. It is every country's right to defend itself, and countries expect to test and improve their defenses against a possible CBW attack.

Defense or attack?

Most industrialized countries have chemical and biological defense programs. The role of these programs is to evaluate the threat that is posed by CBWs and prepare the country's defenses against their possible use. Research into defenses against chemical or biological warfare is allowed under both the **Chemical Weapons Convention (CWC)** and the **Biological Weapons Convention (BWC)** set up by the **UN** (see page 35).

To prepare to defend their country against a CBW attack, scientists have to learn a great deal about how CBWs work. However, this research may open up possibilities for the development of new kinds of chemical or biological weapons. A scientist who is working to help the country's security will be creating knowledge that could be used for making weapons. If a politician decides to turn that knowledge to bad ends, some say it is unfair to blame the scientists.

Part of the job of CBW research scientists is to discover antidotes, medicines that can overcome the effects of CBWs. This is obviously valuable work. However, some people argue that scientists should refuse any CBW research job. But most of us would want to make use of medicines discovered by CBW researchers if there were a CBW attack.

CBW research also tests protective clothing. This man is wearing an **NBC** (nuclear, biological, and chemical) **suit**. He is holding out his hand to prevent people from entering a germ-contaminated area.

This painting shows a child being **vaccinated** against smallpox in the 1820s. Today, researchers work on new antidotes and vaccines, and governments keep supplies of smallpox vaccine ready for use in case of a biological attack.

A dangerous business

Apart from the questions about whether CBW research is right or wrong, the fact that scientists need to work on CBWs in order to do their research creates great risks. The anthrax used in September and October 2001 appears to have been stolen from a U.S. research lab. Some people argue that the risk of such thefts outweighs the benefits of better defense and medical knowledge.

CBW research has sometimes caused human casualties. The center of British CBW research between 1939 and 1989 was a site called Porton Down in southern England. The program there exposed roughly 20,000 "volunteers" to chemical weapons. At the time, many thought they were there to help scientists discover a cure for the common cold, but in fact they were being used for experiments with **nerve agents.** At least one soldier was accidentally killed during nerve gas experiments in 1953 at Porton Down, and others have since claimed to have suffered long-term health effects. However, there has been no hard evidence of this.

Subjects of similar nerve gas experiments in Canada and Australia, who suffered burns and blisters, have recently been awarded **compensation.**

Treaties and Agreements

The United Nations plays a vital role in controlling the use of chemical and biological weapons around the world. This photograph shows members of the UN Security Council voting to approve CBW inspections in Iraq in 2002.

Like any society, a community of nations tries to agree upon and live by laws that are in the best interests of everyone. These international laws go by different names such as treaty, convention, or protocol. They are all contracts signed by politicians on behalf of the nations they represent.

Early agreements

The first known **CBW** warfare treaty was signed between the French and Germans in Strasbourg in 1675. The two nations agreed not to use poisoned bullets in any future war between them.

Two treaties banning the use of poisonous gas were signed in 1874 and 1899 by several powerful nations. But there was very little chance of being found guilty and punished under these laws, because there was no world "police force." Another effort was made in 1925 to create rules that would work better. The Geneva Protocol banned countries from being the first to use CBWs, but not from researching or stockpiling them. It also allowed the nations that had signed the Geneva Protocol to use CBWs against those who had not signed—which included most of the less-developed world.

The Geneva Protocol managed to prevent the use of CBWs in World War II. Because it gave nations the right to strike back against a CBW attack, no country was ready to make the first move and risk this result. But it did nothing to stop CBW research.

Two conventions

By the 1970s, CBW technology was becoming harder to keep secret. In 1972 the **Biological Weapons Convention (BWC)** was agreed upon by leading countries at the **UN** and it came into force in 1975. The BWC outlaws biological weapons, and asks all nations to destroy their stocks and end research into **offensive** weapons. A total of 147 countries have signed up to this treaty.

The **Chemical Weapons Convention (CWC)** was first created in 1993 and came into force in April 1997. By 2003, a total of 151 countries had signed the treaty. The CWC sets out tougher rules than the BWC, and provides a timetable for destroying chemical weapons.

The Australia Group

Side by side with these international agreements, countries work together in other ways to control CBW warfare. The Australia Group is an organization of the world's leading countries, formed to keep an eye on possibly dangerous technology and materials. Together they agree on measures to control the export of certain chemicals, biological **agents,** and **dual-use** materials and technology, so that exports of these items from their countries do not contribute to the increase of CBWs.

During the 1970s, U.S. President Richard Nixon called a halt to most of his country's bioweapons research, inspiring other UN countries to do the same.

Policing the Laws

UN weapons inspectors are viewed through a gateway as they examine a missile factory in Iraq in January 2003.

❝It is simply impractical to declare all potential dual-capable facilities, as these would encompass beer brewers, yogurt makers, and many academic laboratories.❞

Dr. Edward Lacey, U.S. State Department, on possible changes to the BWC

The **Biological Weapons Convention (BWC)** has no police force to back it up. It relies on countries to follow the rules as agreed upon and to police each other. If one country has reason to suspect another of a secret **bioweapons** program, it is up to the countries involved to work out an agreement between themselves or to go to the **UN** to ask for inspections to be arranged.

The **Chemical Weapons Convention (CWC)** is generally thought to have a stronger set of rules than the BWC. It has set up a policing group, the Organization for the Prohibition of Chemical Weapons **(OPCW),** that can launch surprise visits on suspected weapons sites in almost every country in the world.

Site inspections

Site inspections are the best way to prove—or disprove—complaints about a nation's **CBW** program. But it is hard to force a country to agree to an inspection against its will. Countries can and do resist inspections, arguing that their security could be weakened. There can be several reasons for a country wanting to resist inspections. For example, the country being inspected may suspect the inspectors of spying or of stealing CBW secrets to help their own countries' programs. However, measures are in place to guard against the chance of inspections putting national security or trade secrets at risk.

Dual-use checks

Dual-use technology is the toughest nut to crack. The same factory and almost the same materials can be used one week to produce chemical weapons, and the next to make farm fertilizers. Inspection teams have to rely on good information and a sharp eye for detail, such as unusual safety precautions, to discover whether a factory is really manufacturing chemical weapons. This makes the weapons inspectors' job very difficult, and it is possible to make bad mistakes. The Al Shifa medicines factory in East Africa that was bombed by mistake in 1998 (see page 29) was found, after it had been destroyed, to have no airlocks or sealed rooms—both vital precautions for working with CBW materials.

Punishing the Lawbreakers

All the efforts of the organizations for the prohibition of **CBWs** would be pointless if the international community, represented by the **UN,** could not enforce the organizations' decisions. Agreements on the use of CBWs that have failed in the past have done so mainly because they were seen to lack "bite" and to be impossible to enforce. A country that is caught pursuing CBW projects has to be persuaded, or forced, to change its mind. This poses a problem for the UN. On the one hand, it must decide what type of response or punishment is correct. On the other hand, it has to think about the likely bad effects of the UN response on ordinary **civilians** in the country.

Different responses

In the best case, a country's government may be persuaded by careful discussion or negotiation. This approach is called diplomacy, and it provides the least harmful solution. The next level of response is to break off diplomatic relations. This makes the country very isolated. It may also mean that the country misses out on taking part in international decisions on other issues that are important to its future.

A third level of response is for some countries to stop trading with a country. This is known as boycotting, or using sanctions. This response damages the country's economy, but is more likely to harm its poor people than those in power. It also only works against less wealthy economies; few poor countries could afford to boycott rich ones.

The last level is military response. This might simply mean putting armed forces in position to attack. It might also mean bombing a few targets, or it could mean a full-scale war. The military response will result in lost lives and serious damage to property. With all its risks, a military reponse might be the only option if the offending country resists negotiation. The UN needs to have tried all other options before taking actions as serious as this. If CBW laboratories are attacked, they may release poisons into the environment, and this is the opposite of what the **CWC** and **BWC** conventions aim to achieve. The outcome of any military activity is hard to predict.

Military action is the final resort to prevent a government from using chemical or biological weapons. However, war can have terrible consequences for the ordinary people living in the country under attack.

Preparing for the Worst

In addition to signing international agreements to control **CBWs,** governments also work at home to be prepared to deal with CBW warfare. A major part of this work is researching appropriate medical responses to an attack. In the event of a CBW attack, a government needs to be able to do several things quickly. It must find out which CBW has been used, select the best treatment for the victims of the attack, maintain the safety of health care workers, and make sure enough medical resources exist to cope with the attack.

Japanese researchers have recently developed a new type of mask to help protect children from chemical and biological attacks.

Protective measures

CBW research scientists have created new **vaccines** and other medicines to protect people from the effects of CBW warfare. These medicines are kept in storage and soldiers and other people at risk may receive them as a precaution before a CBW attack.

Scientists have developed special equipment to deal with CBW attacks. Armed forces now carry detector equipment that quickly warns soldiers about a CBW attack. Soldiers in danger areas are also issued **NBC suits** ("nuclear, biological, and chemical" suits) to protect them. The U.S. president is followed everywhere by a security team with an NBC suit for him to wear in an emergency.

Safety suits protect soldiers during CBW warfare, but they are very hot to wear. Further testing and training is needed to help soldiers prepare for the extra stresses they will experience in battle when wearing this clothing. Other equipment tested in CBW research programs includes armored vehicles that are CBW-proof.

Coping with a CBW attack

Organizations such as the Red Cross are now able to offer **civilians** detailed advice about how to plan for an emergency and what they can do to help themselves survive CBW attacks. There are also kits available for use in emergencies, containing basic food and first-aid supplies for families.

In addition to developing medicines to fight the effects of CBWs, researchers also study ways of coping with **casualties** who may be "poisonous" to work with. Scientists can give medical staff special training for emergencies. With this knowledge, medical staff can avoid being injured or infected by any leftover CBW on their patients. They can also stop hospitals and ambulances from being **contaminated** while caring for CBW casualties.

Specialized equipment has been developed to deal with CBW attacks. Here, an emergency worker is helped into a protective suit during an anthrax scare in South Africa, October 2001.

Emergency Planning

Military planners use "war games" and exercises to help them discover if their plans will work smoothly. But planning for an attack against **civilians** is a different matter. It is not possible to involve an entire population in a rehearsal. Instead, exercises are invented by experts to test how decision-makers would respond to a crisis.

Case study Dark Winter

In June 2001 experienced U.S. leaders took part in a role-playing exercise to help them think about how they would cope in a worst-case scenario caused by a **CBW** attack. It was held around a conference table on a weekend, and it evolved over a simulated three-week time period. The game was called Dark Winter.

The U.S. leaders pretended that they were all members of a National Security Council (NSC), an organization responsible for making all the important decisions in time of war. The NSC faced a military problem on the Iraq/Kuwait border in the Persian Gulf, but at the first meeting the alarm was raised about a problem much closer to home. There was an outbreak of smallpox in Oklahoma, with twenty known cases of the disease. The NSC agreed to keep some **vaccine** for use by the army, in case this outbreak was caused by some form of CBW attack, and the army was needed to help prevent it from spreading. Remaining stocks of vaccine were sent to affected areas to try to contain the smallpox **virus.**

By week two (in simulated time), 2,000 Americans were infected across fifteen states. The disease was widespread, and vaccine supplies were running out. The president addressed the nation to appeal for calm, but there was panic. People left the cities, carrying the disease with them. Hospitals were flooded with panicking people and casualties, and hospital staff were beginning to leave. Medical services were breaking down.

Soldiers can train to be prepared for a CBW attack. These Russian soldiers are carrying out an exercise in a special training center for CBW protection.

"If you're going against someone who is using a tool that you're not used to having him use—disease—and using it quite rationally and craftily toward an entirely unreasonable and god-awful end—we are in a world we haven't ever really been in before."

R. James Woolsey, former director of the Central Intelligence Agency (CIA) and participant in Dark Winter

Meanwhile, the military crisis in the Persian Gulf was heating up. Could the United States afford to send more troops abroad?

By week three (exercise time), the U.S. public was asking the army to take over and contain the smallpox outbreak, but most of the army was in the Gulf. It was already beyond the power of the police or the National Guard to trace and isolate all the infected people. By now 30,000 were infected, 1,000 were dead, and the experts advised that, in the worst case, another million or so would die before new supplies of vaccine could be delivered. Then a letter from the smallpox **terrorists** arrived, admitting that they had started the outbreak and demanding that the United States pull all forces out of the Gulf, with a threat of further CBW attacks on the United States if they did not. The NSC was in a terrible position, and the United States was forced to consider possible amendments to its emergency CBW defenses.

Nongovernmental Effort

Some organizations concerned with **CBW** warfare are not part of government. They are made up of experts and scientists or members of the public, who try to help reduce the risks of CBWs.

DIPLOMACY NOT BOMBS

Antiwar protesters gather in Canada. Often campaigns against CBWs are carried out "behind the scenes."

AN E
ALL O

Research groups

Some groups of experts and scientists work on producing medicines and treatments to be used if a CBW attack takes place. For example, scientists do research to produce **antibiotics** and **vaccines** that will protect people against CBWs. Other experts develop technologies to give early warning that a CBW attack has taken place so that protective measures can be put into action. Experts and scientists also work on providing emergency management and response plans to reduce the risk posed by attacks.

Other kinds of experts work on chemical and biological warfare issues. These include historians, political scientists, and experts in international law. Historians see how lessons from history can show us what might happen if we do not work to prevent the development of CBWs. Historians, political scientists, and international lawyers look at how international agreements between countries can be strengthened to prevent chemical and biological warfare. Experts and scientists also help members of the public and campaigning organizations who are working to put an end to chemical and biological weapons.

Activist groups

Activist, or campaign, groups intend to bring CBW issues to the top of the heap of issues facing our politicians. They hope to make the problem of CBWs a priority for as many politicians as possible. **Lobby groups** do this quietly by approaching politicians directly, providing them with useful facts and arguments. Other campaign groups tend to make more noise, trying to raise awareness in the media and among voters to get the public to make demands of their politicians, especially at election time. Both types of work need skill and determination to succeed —there are a lot of other issues that compete for public attention.

A few activist groups take direct action to make their point. At this extreme, they may even break laws to publicize the dangers of chemical and biological weapons. For example, they might trespass on a military base to draw attention to secret CBW resources. Members of these groups believe that it is people's moral duty to fight against the use of CBWs, even if this means acting illegally. This sort of campaign is known as civil disobedience, and those who employ it must be ready to accept the legal consequences.

What Are the Risks?

People who are most at risk from **CBWs** can be given **vaccines** to help protect them. Here British soldiers wait to be vaccinated at the start of the 1991 Gulf War.

Most of the information about **CBW** warfare is very frightening, especially after the **terrorist** attacks on the United States in 2001. It can be very hard to make sense of the size of the risk when you read a newspaper headline about "killer germs" on the loose. In 2001 some people were so sure that CBW terrorism was about to happen that they bought medical kits and gas masks for their families. Despite massive media coverage, millions of people did not understand that the risk posed by anthrax was relatively small. But it is easy to be misled about how dangerous something is.

Asking questions

Before people take action, claims about risks have to be carefully considered and a series of questions asked. Who is making the claim? Do they have a rounded view of all the issues? Do other experts agree with the claim? Is there good, solid research to back up the claim? Are the numbers being used vague estimates or solid facts?

CBW warfare poses serious risks if a person has been exposed to CBW material. For example, smallpox kills roughly one in every three infected persons. But it is not correct to calculate from these figures that if there were a smallpox outbreak, one in every three people in a country would die. Not everyone in the country would be infected, and the quality of medical attention that people received, both in protection and treatment, could have a big effect on how the disease affected them.

When journalists describe risks, they often focus on the worst case possible, since it tends to be more interesting. How many times have you heard a news story saying that something is actually pretty safe?

The risk to you from CBW warfare, unless you work in a military research program, is too small to calculate with any accuracy. You can see some figures for comparative risks on page 50 that show just how small the risk is. Your chance of being killed by CBWs is very much less than your chance of being struck by lightning.

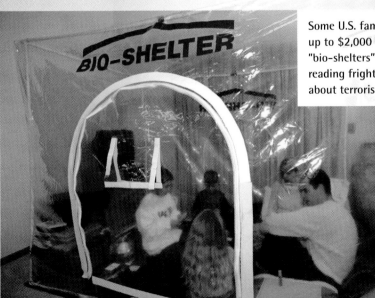

Some U.S. families spent up to $2,000 on plastic "bio-shelters" after reading frightening stories about terrorist attacks.

What Can You Do?

You might feel that your interest in chemistry or biology could be put to use in helping national security efforts. You might want to try to put an end to **CBW** warfare. Or you might think that this issue is not important enough to get worked up about either way.

You and your friends could conduct a survey of public awareness of CBWs. It could be the starting point for some interesting debates.

Each of these viewpoints has good arguments for and against. The first thing you can do is to explore some of the resources at the back of this book to find out more about the subject.

Raising awareness

Awareness of the issue is a good first step, and you might want to check how aware your friends and family are about CBWs. You could just ask them, or you could write out some questions and conduct a survey. Do people know the difference between chemical and biological weapons? Do they know what is allowed by international law and what is forbidden? Do they know which countries have CBW programs? Do they know if their local politician is for or against CBW defense spending? When you have finished, see if you can see any pattern in the responses to your questions. You could also try organizing a debate on CBWs at your school.

If you want to get some people to think further about the topic, try writing letters to your local politicians. Be patient waiting for a reply. You will normally get a personal response within a month or two. You might want to take it further by writing to a newspaper or e-mailing a radio or television station when the issue comes up. Why not write to your local fire and health care services, to ask what plans they have to cope with a CBW emergency?

Take a look at some of the campaign and **lobby groups** listed in the back of the book. Do any of them seem to be doing work that you think deserves some support?

> **❝I know not with what weapons World War III will be fought, but World War IV will be fought with sticks and stones.❞**
>
> The scientist Albert Einstein, predicting that the weapons used in World War III would be so powerfully destructive that humanity would be reduced to living like primitive people once again

Facts and Figures

Counting the human cost

These statistics show the numbers of deaths caused by different types of weapon:

Period	Type of weapon	Numbers killed
1945–1992	conventional weapons	23,000,000
1945–1992	nuclear weapons	absolute estimate impossible; expert opinion gives numbers in low hundreds of thousands
1945–1992	CBW weapons	approx. 100,000

Causes of death

This table lists causes of death in the United States. It shows how extremely small the risk of dying from CBW warfare is:

Heart disease	1 in 385
Accident	1 in 2,928
Homicide (murder)	1 in 14,857
Electrocution	1 in 496,000
Commercial flight accident	1 in 1,568,000
Lightning	1 in 4,288,000
CBW warfare	less than all of the above

Chemical weapons controls

Countries that have declared a weapons program to the **Organization for the Prohibition of Chemical Weapons (OPCW):**

United States
Russia

Countries that have refused the invitation to sign the **Chemical Weapons Convention (CWC):**

North Korea   Egypt
Iraq   Libya
Somalia   Syria

Stores of chemical weapons or chemical weapons factories in the U.S. awaiting destruction

Chemical weapons:

Anniston Army Depot, Alabama; Redstone Arsenal, Alabama; Fort Richardson, Alaska; Pueblo Depot, Colorado; Johnston Atoll, Pacific Ocean; Blue Grass Army Depot, Kentucky; Unatiall Depot, Oregon; Camp Bullis, Texas; Dugway Proving Ground, Utah; Tooele Army Depot, Utah

Chemical weapons factories:

Pine Bluff Arsenal, Arkansas; Rocky Mountain Arsenal, Colorado; Newport Chemical, Indiana; Aberdeen Proving Ground, Maryland

Countries that have not yet signed the Biological Weapons Convention (BWC)

(Note: In many cases, the countries are too small to have a **bioweapons** program)

Andorra	Marshall Islands
Angola	Mauritania
Antigua and Barbuda	Micronesia (Federal States of)
Azerbaijan	Moldova (Republic of)
Cameroon	Mozambique
Chad	Namibia
Comoros	Nauru
Cook Islands	Niue
Djibouti	Palau
East Timor	Samoa, Western
Eritrea	Sudan
Guinea	Tajikistan
Israel	Trinidad and Tobago
Kazakstan	Tuvalu
Kiribati	Zambia
Kyrgyzstan	

Further Information

International contacts

The Australia Group
A nonproliferation organization representing most nations
www.australiagroup.net/index_en.htm

Organization for the Prohibition of Chemical Weapons
Johan de Wittlaan 32, 2517 JR,
The Hague, Netherlands
www.opcw.org
(Warning: history pages may show some disturbing pictures.)

Stockholm International Peace Research Institute (SIPRI)
Signalistgatan 9, SE-169 70 Solna, Sweden
http://projects.sipri.se/cbw/cbw-mainpage.html
Chemical and biological warfare pages
http://cbw.sipri.se/index2.html
A junior educational tour of SIPRI

The Transnational Foundation for Peace and Future Research
Vegagatan 25, S-224 57 Lund, Sweden
e-mail: comments@transnational.org
www.transnational.org
An international network of peace organizations

Contacts in the United States

Center for Civilian Biodefense Strategies
(410) 223-1667
www.hopkins-biodefense.org

Centers for Disease Control and Prevention
1600 Clifton Road, Atlanta, GA 30333
www.bt.cdc.gov
U.S. government bioterror information site

Center for Nonproliferation Studies
460 Pierce Street, Monterey, CA 93940
(831) 647-4154
e-mail: cns@miis.edu
http://cns.miis.edu/research/cbw

Chemical Weapons Convention
U.S. Department of Commerce,
Bureau of Industry and Security,
Treaty Compliance Division,
1555 Wilson Boulevard, Suite 710,
Arlington, VA 22209-2405
www.cwc.gov

Council for a Livable World
110 Maryland Avenue NE,
Washington DC 20002
(202) 543-4100
www.clw.org/involved.html
A U.S. campaigning and **lobby** group

Federation of American Scientists
1717 K St. NW, Suite 209,
Washington DC 20036
(202) 546-3300
www.fas.org/bwc/

Other Internet contacts

www.firstworldwar.com
Archive of information about World War 1

www.nizkor.org
Information on the Holocaust

www.redcross.org/pubs/dspubs/terrormat.html
Advice from the American Red Cross on what to do at home to prepare for CBW warfare

Further reading

Bjornlund, Britta. *The Cold War*. Farmington Hills, Mich.: Gale Group, 2002.

Haugen, David M. *Biological and Chemical Weapons*. Farmington Hills, Mich.: Greenhaven Press, 2001.

Kerrigan, Michael. *Biological and Chemical Warfare Protection*. Broomall, Penn.: Mason Crest, 2002.

Pringle, Laurence. *Chemical and Biological Warfare: The Cruelest Weapons*. Berkeley Heights, NJ: 2000.

Ruleff, Tamara L. *The Holocaust: Death Camps*. Farmington Hills, Mich.: Gale Group, 2001.

Glossary

agent something producing a desired effect

Allies joint forces formed by the United States, Britain, and other countries to fight together on one side in World War I and World War II

ammunition items such as bullets and shells, without which weapons such as guns or tanks are useless

antibiotic medicine that kills bacteria. Different antibiotics affect different types of bacteria.

bacteria single-celled organisms that live in all Earth environments, some of which benefit or harm other life forms

bioweapon weapon that uses life forms to attack an enemy, or the enemy's support systems (such as animals or food crops). Bioweapon is short for biological weapon.

botulinum poison-producing bacteria

casualty person injured or killed in an accident or act of war

Biological Weapons Convention (BWC) international agreement made to outlaw biological weapons

CBW initials standing for chemical and biological weapons. The term CBW is used when talking about both types of weapon at once.

cell basic, microscopic part of a living thing

civilian any person who does not work for the military or security services of a country

Cold War struggle for power between the United States and the Soviet Union, which was at its height in the 1950s and 1960s

communism form of government in which the state owns all means of production, such as factories and farms, and also provides comprehensive social welfare

compensation money paid to someone to make up for harm that has been done to him or her

concentration camp prison camp for civilians who are identified as possible enemies of the state, usually due to their ethnic group

contaminated affected by something dirty or poisonous, such as a CBW. A contaminated object or substance can be very dangerous.

conventional weapons weapons that are not nuclear, chemical, or biological

cult religious group that controls all aspects of its members' lives

Cemical Weapons Convention (CWC) international agreement to outlaw chemical weapons

defoliant chemical that makes leaves fall off plants and trees

delivery system general term for the equipment used to deliver CBW materials to the enemy

disarm to remove weapons or ammunition

dual-use something that has more than one use, for example, machinery or chemical substances that can be used for making CBWs, and also for other purposes such as medicine or agriculture

evacuate to move people away from an area because of danger

fuel-air explosive weapon that is a large canister containing fuels that explode

guerrilla small group of unofficial soldiers who rely on surprise attacks and rapid escape

Kurds people living mainly in northern Iraq, western Iran and eastern Turkey. Many Kurds in Iraq are fighting for their independence and freedom.

lice small wingless insects that live on animals or people

lobby group small political group that campaigns by talking directly to elected politicians

missile weapon delivered on a self-propelled rocket

mustard gas chemical weapon that attacks the lungs and makes the skin blister

NBC suit Nuclear, Biological, and Chemical Suit. All-in-one suit including a gas mask, designed to protect its wearer from nuclear, biological, and chemical warfare.

nerve agent chemical that disables parts of the nervous system, such as the brain. Also called nerve gas.

nuclear weapon bomb or missile that turns matter into energy to cause a massive, powerful explosion

offensive used for attacking, especially as the first move in a conflict

organism general term for any life form

Organization for the Prohibition of Chemical Weapons (OPCW) policing group of the CWC

pesticide chemical designed to kill pests, usually insects

regime system of government

retaliation response to an attack with another attack

Soviet Union (USSR) communist country made up of Russia and its neighbors, formed in 1922 and collapsed in 1991

sterilize to make an object free of bacteria and viruses using X-rays, boiling water, or chemicals such as bleach

Tartars warlike people from central Asia, sometimes also known as Mongols

terrorist someone using violence or fear of violence to achieve political aims

toxin poison

trench deep ditch dug along the front lines on a battlefield, where soldiers can hide from enemy bullets

United Nations (UN) international body set up in 1945 to promote international peace and cooperation

vaccine harmless version of a disease that "teaches" the body to defend itself against that disease. Vaccines are delivered by a process called vaccination.

veteran soldier or ex-soldier who has been involved in a war

Viral Hemorrhagic Fever (VHF) diseases caused by viruses that produce heavy bleeding and fevers, and often are fatal

virus organism that reproduces by "stealing" resources from the cells of other organisms. Many viruses cause diseases.

Index